CONGRATULATIONS
GRADUATE

Honor Books
Tulsa, Oklahoma 74155

Congratulations Graduate
ISBN 1-56292-779-7
Copyright © 2001 by Honor Books
P.O. Box 55388
Tulsa, Oklahoma 74155

INTRODUCTION

Congratulations! You're a graduate. "So now what?" you ask.

Well, there are many decisions to make at this point in your life, so Honor Books has compiled this handy little book for you. *Congratulations Graduate* was designed to do more than just commemorate your achievement. It was created to help you walk confidently down the path toward your future.

In these pages, you'll find tips for job hunting and interviews; quotes that will inspire you and help you focus on what's really important in life; interesting bits of trivia about graduation traditions we all take for granted; and advice, wisdom, and rules for living from those who have "been there, done that."

So take courage! All you need is a little inspiration mixed with some hard work and persistence, and you'll be on your way to success in whatever endeavor you choose to pursue.

*The best thing about the future is that
it comes only one day at a time.*

—Abraham Lincoln

A Blueprint for Achievement

Believe while others are doubting.
Plan while others are playing.
Study while others are sleeping.
Decide while others are delaying.
Prepare while others are daydreaming.
Begin while others are procrastinating.

Work while others are wishing.
Save while others are spending.
Listen while others are talking.
Smile while others are pouting.
Commend while others are criticizing.
Persist while others are quitting.

Job Hunting Tips for Graduates

- Tell everyone you meet about your goals and what you want to do.
- Don't be afraid to pick up the phone and call an employer.
- Always get a contact name.
- Realize there are no perfect interview answers.

- Be persistent.
- Always follow up.
- Treat secretaries and assistants with respect.
- Be yourself.
- Remember: mailing five hundred resumes and waiting for the phone to ring is not a job search.

*A wise person doesn't just wait
for the right opportunity.
They create the right opportunity.*

Get out and Do It!

Get out there and give real help! Get out there and love! Get out there and testify! Get out there and create whatever you can to inspire people to claim their divine being and origin. This is what has to be done now. There is no time. There has never been any time for dallying and being depressed.

—Mother Teresa

I Think I Can

If you think you are beaten, you are;
If you think you dare not, you don't;
If you want to win but think you can't,
It's almost a cinch you won't.
If you think you'll lose, you're lost;
For out in the world we find success
Begins with a fellow's will;
It's all a state of mind.
Life's battles don't always go
To the stronger and faster man,
But sooner or later the man who wins
Is the man who thinks he can.

*Attitude is the master key
to life's little locks.*

Attitude

The longer I live the more I realize the impact of attitude on life. Attitude, to me, is more important than the past, than education, than money, than circumstances, than failures, than success, than what other people think or say or do. It is more important than appearance, giftedness, or skill. It will make or break an organization, a school, a home.

The remarkable thing is we have a choice every day regarding the attitude we will embrace for that day. We cannot change our past. We cannot change the fact that people will act in a certain way. We cannot change the inevitable. The only thing we can do is play the string we have. And that is our attitude. I am convinced that life is 10 percent what happens to me and 90 percent how I react to it. And so it is with you.

—*Charles Swindoll*

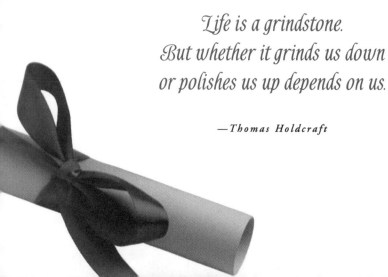

Life is a grindstone.
But whether it grinds us down
or polishes us up depends on us.

—Thomas Holdcraft

Good Advice

Every now and then go away; have a little relaxation. For when you come back to your work, your judgment will be surer, since to remain constantly at work, you lose power of judgment. Go some distance away because then the work appears smaller, and more of it can be taken in at a glance, and a lack of harmony or proportion is more readily seen.

—*Leonardo da Vinci*

Mental Health Rules

1. Have a hobby: acquire pursuits which absorb your interest; sports and nature are best.
2. Develop a philosophy: adapt yourself to social and spiritual surroundings.
3. Share your thoughts: Cultivate companionship in thought and feeling. Confide, confess, consult.
4. Face your fears: analyze them; daylight dismisses ghosts.
5. Balance fantasy with fact: dream, but also do; wish, but build; imagine, but ever face reality.

6. Beware of alluring escapes: alcohol, opiates, and barbitals may prove faithless friends.
7. Exercise: walk, swim, golf; muscles need activity.
8. Love, but love wisely: sex is a flame which uncontrolled may scorch; properly guided, it will light the torch of eternity.
9. Don't become engulfed in a whirlpool of worries: Call early for help. The doctor is ready for your rescue.
10. Trust in time: be patient and hopeful; time is a great therapist.

—Dr. Joseph Fetterman

*As you move through life,
set aside good ideas and give them
to others to encourage and inspire.*

—*Peter J. Daniels*

One of life's great rules is this:
The more you give, the more you get.

—*William H. Danforth*

Go Work!

When God wanted sponges and oysters, He made them and put one on a rock and the other in the mud. When He made man, He did not make him to be a sponge or an oyster; He made him with feet and hands, and head and heart, and vital blood, and a place to use them, and He said to him, "Go work."

—Henry Ward Beecher

Ludwig van Beethoven arose at daybreak and immediately began composing until 2 P.M. when he would have dinner. He worked in long stretches of unbroken time to allow his thoughts to unfold and flow uninterrupted. He exemplified a bias for action.

John Wesley, the founder of Methodism, traveled more than 250,000 miles on horseback, preaching often fifteen times a week for over fifty years. As an octogenarian, he complained that he found it difficult to work more than fifteen hours a day.

—C. T. Winchester

Persistence

Nothing in the world can take the place of persistence. Talent will not; nothing is more common than unsuccessful people with talent. Genius will not; unrewarded genius is almost a proverb. Education will not; the world is full of educated failures. Keep believing. Keep trying. Persistence and determination alone are omnipotent.

—*Calvin Coolidge*

You may even have to hang on after others have let go. Persistence means taking pains to overcome every obstacle, to do all that's necessary to reach your goal. In the end, the only people who fail are those who do not try. All great achievements take time.

Stand your ground, and after you have done everything. . . . Stand firm then.

Ephesians 6:13-14

I'm a slow walker, but I never walk back.

—*Abraham Lincoln*

March to Your Own Beat

If one advances confidently in the direction of his dreams, and endeavors to live the life which he has imagined, he will meet with a success unexpected in common hours. . . . Why should we be in such desperate haste to succeed, and in such desperate enterprises? If a man does not keep pace with his companions, perhaps it is because he hears a different drummer. Let him step to the music which he hears, however measured or far away.

—Henry David Thoreau

Did You Know?

The robes worn by graduating students in today's commencement ceremonies were once the normal dress code in the universities of twelfth-century Europe. Robes and hoods were worn by clerics, whether students or teachers, because the classrooms and hallways were so drafty and cold. There was no such thing as central heating in those days.

First Home

Here are just a few things you'll need when setting up housekeeping for the first time:

1. Appliances—TV, coffeemaker, and microwave.

2. Furniture—bed, couch, dining table, and chairs.

3. Cookware—pots, pans, silverware, plates, bowls, glasses, and cups.

4. Linens—towels, washcloths, sheets, blankets, pillows and pillowcases.

Don't Be Afraid to Fail

You've failed many times, although you may not remember. You fell down the first time you tried to walk. You almost drowned the first time you tried to swim, didn't you? Did you hit the ball the first time you swung a bat? Heavy hitters, the ones who hit the most home runs, also strike out a lot.

R. H. Macy failed 7 times before his store in New York caught on. English novelist John Creasey got 753 rejection slips before he published 564 books. Babe Ruth struck out 1,330 times, but he also hit 714 home runs. Don't worry about failure. Worry about the chances you miss when you don't even try.

—Published in the Wall Street Journal

Steps for Choosing a Career

1. Begin with your values: What's really important to you? What do you like to do so much that you would almost feel guilty getting paid to do it? These questions are designed to help you reach one of the key elements in career choice: values.

2. Identify your skills and talents: A skill is something you've learned to do. A talent is something you've been born with, or at least that you seem naturally qualified to do.

3. Experiment: There's no substitute for experience, the more the better. Take a job in the field or industry and see for yourself if it's really all you thought it would be.

4. Become broadly literate: Learn as much as you can about what interests you and about the jobs and careers you're considering.

5. In your first job, opt for experience first, money second.

6. Aim for a job in which you can become 110 percent committed: Modest commitment and average performance are unacceptable today. If you aren't able to commit 110 percent to what you are currently doing, start NOW to find something to which you can.

7. Build your lifestyle around your income, not your expectations.

8. Invest 5 percent of your time, energy, and money into furthering your career.

9. Be willing to change and adapt.

On the Subject of Money

Money will buy a bed, but not sleep;
books, but not brains;
food, but not appetite;
finery, but not beauty;
a house, but not a home;
medicine, but not health;
luxuries, but not culture;
amusement, but not happiness;
religion, but not salvation;
and a passport to everywhere but Heaven.

*A man's treatment of money is the most decisive test
of his character—how he makes it and how he spends it.*

—*James Moffatt*

*But thou shalt remember the LORD thy God:
for it is he that giveth thee power to get wealth,
that he may establish his covenant which he sware
unto thy fathers, as it is this day.*

Deuteronomy 8:18 KJV

*To challenge yourself is no different
than to give yourself a chance.*

Take a Chance

There is a tide in the affairs of men,
Which, taken at the flood, leads on to fortune;
Omitted, all the voyage of their life
Is bound in shallows and in miseries.
On such a full sea are we not afloat;
And we must take the current when it serves,
Or lose our ventures.

—William Shakespeare
(Brutus in Julius Caesar)

In order to succeed,
we must first believe that we can.

Confidence is assurance that God is with you in whatever you do or say.

"Lo, I am with you alway, even *unto the end of the world."*

Matthew 28:20 KJV

A Model of Integrity

The finals of the U.S. Amateur Golf Championship of 1997 were one of the most exciting and dramatic golf events of the year. Playing in the finals were Steve Scott and Tiger Woods. On the eighteenth green, the final hole, Steve was one up, putting first. Tiger's ball was in Steve's putting line, so Tiger spotted his ball a club-head length away and marked it. Steve Scott putted and missed.

Tiger carefully circled the green, viewed every possible angle, and was lined up to putt when Steve reminded him that he had not spotted his ball back in the original spot. Making the correction, Tiger sank the putt, and the match was thrown into "sudden death," which was won by Tiger Woods.

Here's the reason Steve Scott is such a marvelous role model. Had he not reminded Tiger that he had not respotted his ball correctly, and Tiger had stroked the putt, he would have been penalized two strokes and lost the championship.

—Zig Ziglar

Progress comes from the intelligent use of experience.

—*Elbert Hubbard*

Did You Know?

The ceremonial mace traditionally carried by the president of a university was originally a heavy, often-spiked club used in the Middle Ages to break armor. Medieval bishops carried maces rather than swords because they were forbidden by church law to shed blood. The earliest ceremonial maces were used in England during the reign of Richard I and were carried by the sergeants at arms—royal bodyguards. Maces symbolizing royal authority were constructed of gold, silver, and precious jewels. Today they are widely used at commencements, legislative sessions, and in ecclesiastic ceremonies. Colleges and universities adopted the tradition of carrying a mace as a symbol of the authority to confer academic degrees and honors.

Words of Wisdom

Make new friends, but cherish the old ones.
Don't use time or words carelessly; neither can be retrieved.
Judge your success by the degree that you're enjoying peace, health, and love.
Smile a lot: It costs nothing yet is beyond priceless.

Remember that time is money.

—*Benjamin Franklin*

Cover-letter Tips

Limit yourself to one page. Most cover letters consist of the following three paragraphs:

- Paragraph 1: a brief introduction of yourself, including a description of your career objective.

- Paragraph 2: a short description of your education, skills, and other relevant information.

- Paragraph 3: a closing paragraph, indicating your salary requirements, contact address, and contact number. Also include your e-mail address and fax number if available.

Resumé Tips

Writing your first resumé can seem like a scary prospect at first, but these tips can help you get started:

1. Think of your resumé as an advertisement—you are the product.

2. Match the style of your resumé to the position/company you are applying for.

3. Always be honest about your experience and achievements. Don't overstate, but don't sell yourself short either.

4. A resumé should never be more than one page unless you have extensive experience; in that case, key points should always be on the first page.

5. Clearly state your objective in one well-written sentence.

6. Remember, if you get stuck, there are many resources available. Check out books at the library, or go online.

*Yesterday is not ours to recover,
but tomorrow is ours to win or to lose.*

—Lyndon B. Johnson

Winner vs. Loser

The winner is always part of the answer. The loser is always part of the problem. The winner always has a program. The loser always has an excuse. The winner says, "Let me do it for you." The loser says, "That's not my job." The winner sees an answer for every problem. The loser sees a problem for every answer. The winner sees a green near every sand trap. The loser sees two or three sand traps near every green. The winner says, "It may be difficult, but it's possible." The loser says, "It may be possible, but it's too difficult." Be a winner.

*Small opportunities are often
the beginning of great enterprises.*

—Demosthenes

If the opportunity exists, I will find it.
If not, I will create it.

The Ship That Sails

I'd rather be the ship that sails and rides the billows wild and free;
Than to be the ship that always fails to leave its port and go to sea.
I'd rather feel the sting of strife, where gales are born and tempests roar;
Than settle down to useless life and rot in dry dock on the shore.

I'd rather fight some mighty wave with honor in supreme command;
And fill at last a well-earned grave, than die in ease upon the sand.
I'd rather drive where sea storms blow, and be the ship that always failed
to make the ports where it would go, than be the ship that never sailed.

Things to Do with Your Graduation Cap

1. Use it as a painter's palette.
2. Play Frisbee with it.
3. Wear it upside down to collect rainwater.
4. Pretend it's a satellite dish or TV antenna.
5. Make it into a fashionable chip 'n' dip holder.

Things to Do with Your Tassel

1. Use it for a computer keyboard cleaner.
2. Tie it on a kite for a tail.
3. Use it as a pull for your ceiling fan.
4. Out of dental floss? No problem!
5. Make it into a fancy bookmark.

*Patience: The ability to accept
and remain calm in difficult situations.*

*Strengthened with all might, according to his glorious power,
unto all patience and longsuffering with joyfulness.*

Colossians 1:11 KJV

*Life's challenges are not supposed
to paralyze you; they're supposed
to help you discover who you are.*

Opportunity Knocks?

What is opportunity, and when does it knock? It never knocks. You can wait a whole lifetime, listening, hoping, and you will hear no knocking—none at all. You are opportunity, and you must knock on the door leading to your destiny. So prepare yourself to recognize opportunity. Pursue and seize it as you develop strong character and build a self-image worthy of respect.

If you want to succeed in the world, you must create your own opportunities. The ones who wait for some seventh wave to toss them on dry land will find that the seventh wave is a long time a'coming. You can commit no greater folly than to sit by the roadside until someone comes along and invites you to ride with him or her to wealth or influence.

*No matter how long it takes,
if you keep moving, one step at a time,
you will reach the finish line.*

Each day is another step in your life's journey.

—*Josh S. Hinds*

Some people succeed because they are destined to, but most people succeed because they are determined to.

Four steps to achievement:
plan purposefully,
prepare prayerfully,
proceed positively,
pursue persistently.

—*William Arthur Ward*

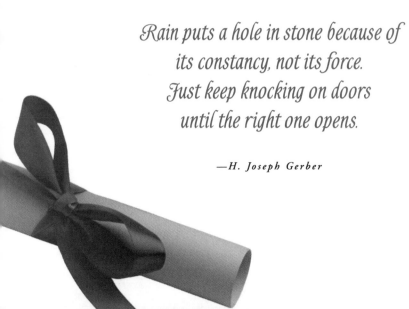

*Rain puts a hole in stone because of
its constancy, not its force.
Just keep knocking on doors
until the right one opens.*

—H. Joseph Gerber

*If at first you don't succeed,
try reading the instructions.*

*Take fast hold of instruction; let her not go:
keep her; for she is thy life.*

Proverbs 4:13 KJV

Interview Tips

The following things are good to remember while preparing for your job interview:

1. Know yourself.
2. Dress appropriately.
3. Be honest.
4. Be positive.
5. Demonstrate interest.
6. Negotiate salary.
7. Follow-up.

First interviews are the initial impressions.
Closing an interview is a lasting impression.

The great composer does not set to work because he is inspired, but becomes inspired because he is working. Beethoven, Wagner, Bach, and Mozart settled down day after day to the job in hand with as much regularity as an accountant settles down each day to his figures. They didn't waste time waiting for an inspiration.

—*Ernest Newman*

It is difficult to steer a parked car, so get moving.

—*Henrietta Mears*

*Do not merely listen to the word, and
so deceive yourselves. Do what is says.*

James 1:22

A Step of Faith

A man once went for a ride in the country with a friend. They drove off the main road and through a grove of orange trees to a mostly uninhabited piece of land. Walter stopped the car and began to vividly describe the things he was going to build on the land. He explained to his friend, "I can handle the main project myself. It will take all my money, but I want you to have the first chance at this surrounding acreage because in the next five years it will increase in value several hundred times."

Arthur thought to himself, *Who in the world is going to drive twenty-five miles for this crazy project? His dream has taken the best of his common sense.* He promised to look into the deal later.

"Later on will be too late," Walter cautioned. "You'd better move on it right now."

Arthur failed to act, however. And so it was that Art Linkletter turned down the opportunity to buy the land that surrounded what would become Disneyland, the land his friend Walt Disney had tried to talk him into buying. When opportunity greets you, sometimes you have to take a step of faith.

All glory comes from daring to begin.

Dwight L. Moody was a man of action. Once he mentioned a clever promotion idea to a church leader and asked, "What do you think?"

"We've been aimin' to do it for two years," the layman replied.

"Well, now," Moody retorted, "don't you think it's time to fire?"

—George Sweeting

Life is a hard fight, a struggle, a wrestling with the principle of evil, hand to hand, foot to foot. Every inch of the way is disputed. The night is given us to take breath, to pray, to drink deep at the fountain of power. The day, to use the strength which has been given us, to go forth to work with it till the evening.

—*Florence Nightingale*

Life is not advancement. It is growth. It does not move upward, but expands outward, in all directions.

I pray that your love for each other will overflow more
and more, and that you will keep on growing
in your knowledge and understanding.

Philippians 1:9 NLT

*Courage is the strength from God that
enables you to endure any trial or danger.*

*Be strong and courageous. Do not be afraid or terrified
because of them, for the LORD your God goes with you;
he will never leave you nor forsake you.*

Deuteronomy 31:6

When it is dark enough, men see the stars.

—*Ralph Waldo Emerson*

Ideals

The power of ideals is incalculable. We see no power in a drop of water. But let it get into a crack in the rock and be turned to ice, and it splits the rock; turned into steam, it drives the pistons of the most powerful engines. Something has happened to it which makes active and effective the power that is latent in it.

—*Albert Schweitzer*

*First thing every morning before you arise
say out loud, "I believe," three times.*

Never tell a young person that something cannot be done.
God may have been waiting for countless
centuries for somebody ignorant enough
of the impossibility to do that thing.

*And God gives to every man the virtue,
temper, understanding, taste, that lifts him into life
and lets him fall just in the niche he was ordained to fill.*

—*William Cowper*

*I will instruct you and teach you in the way you
should go; I will counsel you and watch over you.*

Psalm 32:8

Opportunities for Success Are around You

Success doesn't come to you; you have to go to it. It's up to you to open the door to opportunity. The golden opportunity you are seeking is inside of you. It is not in your environment; it is not in chance or luck or the help of others; it is inside of you alone. You can start precisely where you are at any time.

The grass always looks greener in far away places, but opportunity lies right where you are. Take advantage of it when it appears. You don't need more strength, more ability, or greater opportunity. What you need is to use what you have. Learn to seize good fortune, for it is always around you. Every situation, properly perceived, becomes an opportunity. The real challenge in life is to choose, hold, and operate through intelligent, uplifting, and fully empowering beliefs.

—Michael Sky

Remind yourself regularly that you are better than you think you are. Successful people are not superhuman. Success does not require a super-intellect. Nor is there anything mystical about success. Success isn't based on luck. Successful people are just ordinary individuals who have developed belief in themselves and their endeavors. Never—yes, never—sell yourself short.

The entire ocean is affected by a pebble.

—*Blaise Pascal*

A man leaves all kinds of footprints when he walks through life. Some you can see, like his children and his house. Others are invisible, like the prints he leaves across other people's lives: the help he gives them and what he has said—his jokes, gossip that has hurt others, encouragement. A man doesn't think about it, but everywhere he passes, he leaves some kind of mark.

—Margaret Lee Runbeck

Life is like a game of cards.
The hand you are dealt is determinism;
the way you play it is free will.

What God Can Do

If God can make of an ugly seed,
with a bit of earth and air
and dew and rain, sunshine and shade,
a flower so wondrous and fair.
What can He make of a soul like you,
with the Bible and faith and prayer,
and the Holy Spirit, if you do His will
and trust in His love and care.

God does not ask about our ability, but our availability.

I can do all things through Christ who strengthens me.

—Philippians 4:13 NKJV

Top Ten Tips for Relieving Stress

1. Slow down. A slower pace may decrease your rush of adrenaline and calm down your body physically.
2. Schedule early morning appointments. This will eliminate or minimize the chance of having to spend time waiting for the appointment.
3. Reduce phone time. If you find it difficult to cut off conversation with particular people, try telling them at the beginning of the call how busy you are.
4. Rent a funny video.
5. Play a game.

6. Read. Find an enjoyable novel, and let it take you away.
7. Wake up thirty minutes earlier than usual, and enjoy the free half hour of time.
8. Allow twice as long as you think you need for getting places or completing projects.
9. Get a massage!
10. Let someone else drive. Carpool, or take public transportation. Sit back, and enjoy conversation, music, reading, or even a nap.

More Interview Tips

The following qualities will enhance your ability to come across professionally and effectively in an interview:

1. Excellent communication skills
2. Confidence
3. Amiable personality
4. Sense of accomplishment
5. Knowledge

Always go to an interview with a confident attitude. The more you tend to think you can't, the more your mind weakens, and the less you can. So tell yourself you can and you will. There is a job out there for everyone. Don't give up! No one was born knowing everything. It's okay to make mistakes.

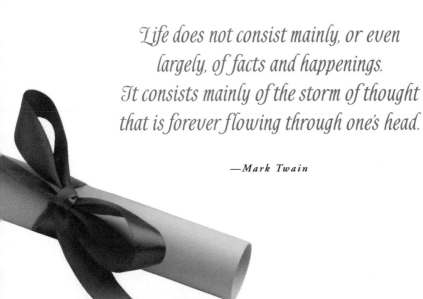

*Life does not consist mainly, or even
largely, of facts and happenings.
It consists mainly of the storm of thought
that is forever flowing through one's head.*

—*Mark Twain*

Imagination

When I could not sleep for cold,
I had fire enough in my brain,
and built with roofs of gold
my beautiful castles in Spain!

—James Russell Lowell

*I like the dreams of the future better
than the history of the past.*

—Thomas Jefferson

Trust the unknown future to the known God.

So do not fear, for I am with you; do not be dismayed,
for I am your God. I will strengthen you and help you;
I will uphold you with my righteous right hand.

Isaiah 41:10

True Success

Success: To laugh often and much; to win the respect of intelligent people and the affection of children; to earn the appreciation of honest critics and endure the betrayal of false friends; to appreciate beauty; to find the best in others; to leave the world a bit better, whether by a healthy child, a garden patch, or a redeemed social condition; to know even one life has breathed easier because you have lived. This is to have succeeded!

—*Ralph Waldo Emerson*

*If you have no critics,
you'll likely have no success.*

The common idea that success spoils people by making them vain, egotistic, and self-complacent is erroneous; on the contrary, it makes them, for the most part, humble, tolerant, and kind. Failure makes people cruel and bitter.

—W. Somerset Maugham

As in nature, as in art, so in grace; it is rough treatment that gives souls, as well as stones, their lustre. The more the diamond is cut, the brighter it sparkles; and in what seems hard dealing, there God has no end in view but to perfect His people.

—Thomas Guthrie

*The more you study,
the more you get paid.*

*No one ever attains very eminent success by
simply doing what is required of him;
it is the amount and excellence of what is over
and above the required that determines
the greatness of ultimate distinction.*

—*Charles Kendall Adams*

God's Farm

The universe is God's farm, and the people of the world are all seeds of sorts, sewn by God to ripen when the time is right. There are five challenges you must face, which is necessary for growth: Love God above all else. Love others as yourself. Work hard, using your talents for good. Enjoy life and all that you do. Accept all pain as lessons when they come and learn from them.

—*Philip St. Romain*

Rules to Live By

1. Laugh at yourself and at life.
2. Never neglect the little things.
3. Welcome every morning with a smile.
4. Set goals for each day—not long and difficult projects—but small chores that will take you, step by step, toward your dream.

Just because something doesn't do what you planned it to do doesn't mean it's useless.

—*Thomas Alva Edison*

When you come to the end of your rope . . .
tie a knot and hang on.

—*Franklin D. Roosevelt*

We consider blessed those who have persevered.
You have heard of Job's perseverance and have seen
what the Lord finally brought about. The Lord
is full of compassion and mercy.

James 5:11

Goals are the result of bringing dreams, ideas, and ideals into tangible and examinable form.

—Peter J. Daniels

We grow great by dreams. All big men are dreamers. They see things in the soft haze of a spring day or in the red fire of a long winter's evening. Some of us let these great dreams die, but others nourish and protect them; nurse them through bad days till they bring them to the sunshine and light which comes always to those who sincerely hope that their dreams will come true.

—Woodrow Wilson

Do You Know Where You're Going?

One day a traveler in a remote country town, convinced that he was on the wrong road, came to a halt in a village. Calling one of the villagers to the car window, he said, "Friend, I need help. I'm lost."

The villager looked at him for a moment. "Do you know where you are?" he asked.

"Yes," said the traveler. "I saw the name of your town as I entered."

The man nodded his head, "Do you know where you want to be?"

"Yes," the traveler replied.

"You're not lost," he said. "You just need directions."

Many of us are in the same position as that traveler. We know where we are—sometimes disappointed, dissatisfied, and experiencing little peace of mind. And we know where we want to be—at peace, fulfilled, and living life abundantly. Like the traveler, we are not lost—we just need directions.

—Zig Ziglar

*I expect to spend the rest of my life
in the future, so I want to be reasonably
sure what kind of future it's going to be.
That is my reason for planning.*

—*Charles F. Kettering*

*There are dreamers and there are planners;
the planners make their dreams come true.*

A Place of Your Own

Moving into a place of your own is a big step. You will need to think about the following things:

1. Cost—How much can you afford to pay each month?

2. Type—What kind of housing do you want?

3. Tenure—Do you want to own or rent?

4. Location—Do you need to live close to work, school, shops, or public transportation?

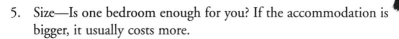

5. Size—Is one bedroom enough for you? If the accommodation is bigger, it usually costs more.

6. Start-up costs—Can you afford a deposit and payment in advance? What about the cost of having the electricity, gas, and phone connected? What about furniture and appliances?

7. Ongoing costs—Remember that as well as paying for your housing, you also need to pay for food, gas, electricity, and personal items such as clothes, entertainment, and transportation.

*In the long run, you hit only what you aim at.
Therefore, though you should fail immediately,
you had better aim at something high.*

—*Henry David Thoreau*

*You must have long-range goals
to keep you from being frustrated
by short-range failures.*

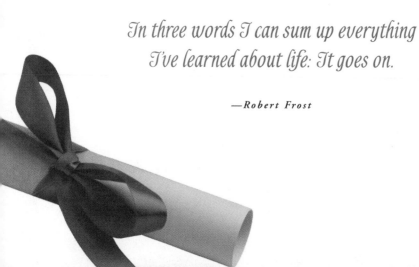

*In three words I can sum up everything
I've learned about life: It goes on.*

—Robert Frost

Did You Know?

The flat cap or mortarboard worn by graduates during commencement originated at Oxford University in England. The tassel is usually the same color as the cap and gown for high school seniors, but at the university level, it traditionally reflects the color assigned to the graduate's area of study.

*Nurture your thoughts with great thoughts;
to believe in the heroic makes heroes.*

There are only two ways to live your life.
One is as though nothing is a miracle.
The other is as though everything is a miracle.

—Albert Einstein

Originality does not consist in saying what no one has ever said before, but in saying exactly what you think yourself.

to be nobody but yourself—in a world which is doing its best, night and day, to make you like everybody else—means to fight the hardest battle which any human being can fight, and never stop fighting.

—*e. e. cummings*

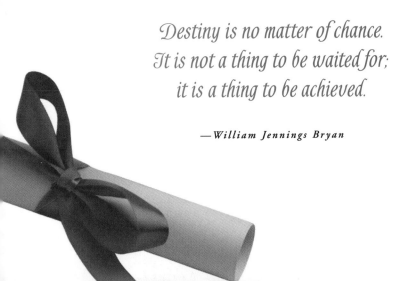

Destiny is no matter of chance.
It is not a thing to be waited for;
it is a thing to be achieved.

—*William Jennings Bryan*

Success isn't something you chase.
It's something you have to put
forth the effort for constantly.
Then it'll come when you least expect it.

—*Michael Jordan*

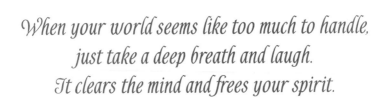

When your world seems like too much to handle,
just take a deep breath and laugh.
It clears the mind and frees your spirit.

*The rainbows of life
follow the storm.*

Don't cross your bridges until you get to them.
We spend our lives defeating ourselves
crossing bridges we never get to.

—*Bob Bates*

Yesterday is but a dream. Tomorrow is only a vision.
But today well lived, makes every yesterday a dream
of happiness and every tomorrow a vision of hope.
Look well, therefore, to this day.

Key Skills

The following are key skills that employers are looking for (to a greater or lesser extent depending on the job):

1. Motivational—affects others positively
2. Sociable—social confidence, outgoing nature
3. Communicative—communicates eloquently
4. Competitive—desires or needs to win
5. Task oriented—desires to achieve deadlines or tasks
6. Initiative—instigates, shapes, and develops tasks
7. Decisive—assesses and takes risks

8. Influential—has a level of authority and leadership
9. Sensitive—is aware of the needs of others
10. Determined—demands from self and others
11. Cooperative—works toward group goals
12. Data focused—enjoys working with data
13. Innovative—enjoys creative, unstructured work
14. Methodical—enjoys repetitive, structured work
15. People focused—enjoys interaction with people

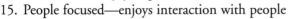

*Punctuality: Being on time
for the requirements of life.*

To every thing there is *a season, and a time
to every purpose under the heaven.*

Ecclesiastes 3:1 KJV

We all start out in life with one thing in common—we all have the same amount of time. It's just a matter of what we do with it.

—Harvey B. Mackay

If a task is once begun, never leave it
till it's done. Be the labor great
or small, do it well or not at all.

Doing your best: Putting your whole mind, body, and soul into the task at hand.

And whatsoever ye do, do it heartily, as to the Lord, and not unto men.

Colossians 3:23 KJV

An Interview Tip

At some time during the interview process, always mention to the prospective employer that everywhere you have been employed you have been part of the solution and not part of the problem.

After the Interview

Always send a thank-you letter to your interviewer within twenty-four hours of the interview. The letter gives you a chance to reiterate the reasons you are a good candidate and point out other important qualities you forgot to mention. It also marks you as a professional, appreciative of the time spent by your interviewer.

I Can Make or Break You

I am your constant companion. I am your greatest helper or heaviest burden. I will push you onward and upward or drag you down to failure. I am completely at your command. Ninety percent of the things you do might just as well be turned over to me, and I will be able to do them quickly and correctly. I am easily managed. Show me exactly how you want something done, and after a few lessons, I will do it automatically.

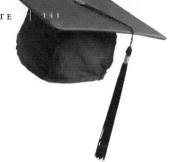

I am the servant of all great people, and alas, of all failures as well. I am not a machine, though I work with all the precision of a machine, plus the intelligence of a human being. You can run me for profit or run me for ruin—it makes no difference to me. Take me, train me, be firm with me, and I will place the world at your feet. Be easy with me, and I will destroy you. Who am I? I am a habit.

*Tact: The ability to describe others
as they see themselves.*

—Abraham Lincoln

Personality can open doors,
but only character can keep them open.

—Elmer G. Leterman

*Life is like a piano—
what you get out of it,
depends on how you play it.*

A Creed for Life

To be so strong that nothing can disturb your peace of mind; to talk health, happiness, and prosperity; to make your friends feel that there is something in them; to look on the sunny side of everything; to think only of the best; to be just as enthusiastic about the success of others as you are about your own; to forget the mistakes of the past and profit by them; to wear a cheerful countenance and give a smile to everyone you meet; to be too large for worry, too noble for anger, too strong for fear, and too happy to permit the presence of trouble.

—*Christian D. Larson*

The Importance of Fitness

The joy of feeling fit physically is reflected in a clearer and more useful mind. You may read and study forever, but you come to no more important truthful conclusions than these two: (1) Take care of your body (eat and exercise properly), and your mind will improve. (2) Work hard and be polite and fair, and your condition in the world will improve.

No pills, tablets, lotions, philosophies will do as much for you as this simple formula I have outlined. The formula is not of my invention. Every intelligent man of experience since time began has taught it as a natural fact.

—*Edgar Watson Howe*

You can change your beliefs so they empower your dreams and desires. Create a strong belief in yourself and what you want.

Resolved: To live with all my might while I do live.

Resolved: Never to lose one moment of time, to improve it in the most profitable way I possibly can.

Resolved: Never to do anything which I should despise or think meanly of in another.

Resolved: Never to do anything out of revenge.

Resolved: Never to do anything which I should be afraid to do if it were the last hour of my life.

—Jonathan Edwards

Dependability:
Being reliable and trustworthy
to do what you say you will do.

"'Well done, good and faithful servant!
You have been faithful with a few things;
I will put you in charge of many things.'"

Matthew 25:21

Responsibility:
The reliability or trustworthiness
to do what is expected of you.

So then, each of us will give an account of himself to God.

Romans 14:12

The only thing that stands between people and what they want from life is often merely the will to try it and the faith to believe that it is possible.

*To accomplish great things, we must not only act,
but also dream; not only plan, but also believe.*

Leap of Faith

A young man who was disconcerted about the uncertainty of his future, sat in a park, watching squirrels scamper among the trees. Suddenly a squirrel jumped from one high tree to another. It appeared to be aiming for a limb so far out of reach that the leap looked like suicide. As the young man expected, the squirrel missed its mark—but it landed, safe and unconcerned—on a branch several feet lower. Then it climbed to its goal, and all was well.

An old man sitting on the other end of the bench remarked, "Funny, I've seen hundreds of 'em jump like that, especially when there are dogs around, and they can't come down to the ground. A lot of 'em miss, but I've never see any hurt in trying." Then he chuckled and added, "I guess they've got to risk it if they don't want to spend their lives in one tree."

Love work.
Turn a deaf ear to slander.
Do not be taken up by trifles.
Do not resent plain speaking.
Meet offenders half way.
Be thorough in thought.
Have an open mind.
Do your duty without grumbling.

—Marcus Aurelius

A Prayer for the Graduate

May you have enough happiness to keep you sweet, trials to keep you strong, sorrow to keep you human, hope to keep you happy, failure to keep you humble, success to keep you eager, friends to give you comfort, wealth to meet your needs, enthusiasm to keep you looking forward, faith to banish depression, and determination to make each day better than yesterday.

Additional copies of this book and other titles
for graduates are available from your local bookstore.

If you have enjoyed this book, or if it has
impacted your life, we would like to hear from you.
Please contact us at:

Honor Books
Department E
P.O. Box 55388
Tulsa, Oklahoma 74155
Or by e-mail at *info@honorbooks.com*

Honor Books
Tulsa, Oklahoma